MW01129350

I NEED TO
LOVE OTHER
PEOPLE

GOD AND ME

BOOKS IN SERIES

I Need to Trust in God
I Need to Hope in God
I Need to Love God
I Need to Love Other People

I NEED TO LOVE OTHER PEOPLE

Joel and Mary Beeke

Illustrated by Cassandra Clark

Reformation Heritage Books
Grand Rapids, Michigan

I Need to Love Other People
© 2021 by Joel and Mary Beeke

All rights reserved. No part of this book may be used or reproduced in any manner whatsoever without written permission except in the case of brief quotations embodied in critical articles and reviews. Direct your requests to the publisher at the following addresses:

Reformation Heritage Books
3070 29th St. SE
Grand Rapids, MI 49512
616-977-0889
orders@heritagebooks.org
www.heritagebooks.org

Printed in China
21 22 23 24 25 26/10 9 8 7 6 5 4 3 2 1

Library of Congress Cataloging-in-Publication Data

Names: Beeke, Joel R., 1952– author. | Beeke, Mary, author. | Clark, Cassandra, illustrator.
Title: I need to love other people / Joel and Mary Beeke ; illustrated by Cassandra Clark.
Description: Grand Rapids, Michigan : Reformation Heritage Books, [2021] | Series: God and me | Audience: Ages 4–7
Identifiers: LCCN 2021002920 | ISBN 9781601788726 (hardcover)
Subjects: LCSH: Caring—Religious aspects—Christianity—Juvenile literature. | Golden rule— Juvenile literature. | Love—Biblical teaching—Juvenile literature.
Classification: LCC BV4647.S9 B44 2021 | DDC 241/.4—dc23
LC record available at https://lccn.loc.gov/2021002920

For additional Reformed literature, request a free book list from Reformation Heritage Books at the above regular or email address.

MEMORY VERSE

"Thou shalt love thy neighbor as
thyself" (Matthew 22:39).

Noah was the new kid.

He was in second grade with Caleb and his friend Logan.

Bb
Cc
Ee
Ff
Hh
Jj
MEDITERRANEAN SEA
LOWER EGYPT
UPPER EGYPT
RED SEA

"God told the Israelites to love new people, because they themselves used to be strangers in Egypt."

"God told them to leave grapes and grain for those who didn't have enough."

"Love God above all, and love your neighbor as yourself."

"Hey, Logan. It's bothering me that those big kids were mean to Noah, and we didn't do anything."

"Noah, want a granola bar?"

"Hey Noah, want to be on our team?"

"It is wonderful to love other people."

TALK ABOUT IT

1. What did Jesus mean when He said that in everything we do, we are to treat other people the way we would like to be treated (see Matthew 7:12)?

2. How can you love others by praying for them and showing them kindness?

Note to parents: Jesus loved people. When the Holy Spirit plants His love in our hearts, we will love our neighbor, too. That includes everyone who crosses our path in God's providence. Explain to your children that we need God to teach us to love all kinds of people as we love ourselves. When this happens, we will care for them and want what is best for them.